Love and other nuances from my write hand

Shiane Wilcoxen

BookLeaf Publishing

Presentation by *BookLeaf Publishing*

Web: www.bookleafpub.com

E-mail: info@bookleafpub.com

ISBN: 9789358314038

First edition 2023

I dedicate this to my Son, DominiQuinn Edmund Wilcoxen who has been my sole reason to keep pushing through life since May 21, 2003. Without you my beautiful boy, I would have never made it this far. You are my oxygen. I love you more than peanut butter.

ACKNOWLEDGEMENT

To the bold, fierce, courageous lesbians of this world, I love you all. Thank you to those that came before me and fought for my own autonomy and freedom to live my authentic self. To my Aunties, and Mommas, and Sistahs "in the life", thank you for raising me and guiding me through and helping me become the woman that I am today. To the women of Chicago's POW-WOW at Jeffrey Pub that took in a little, lost, fresh out of the closet lesbian and made me your family, I love you; I salute you. I honor you.

PREFACE

All of the feelings and emotions in this book really occurred. I can't name each and every woman that I wrote these words for, because I rather not remember some of them. But all in all, I lived, I loved, I did not laugh. But I am still standing on my own two feet and continue to believe in true love everlasting.

My write hand

These sheets of paper. This pen. My hand swift. My mind sharp. Eyes welling with tears. Reaching in and ripping muscle and veins. Blood and salty tears. Tearing my heart our and putting it in between these lines. It's messy. But she needs to see it. The heart speaks. And now I write. Heart. Lust. Confusion. Blinded my judgment. Glad my mind quickly allowed my common sense to recover. But my heart strings have already been stretched beyond repair. Inconsolable. Should have known I couldn't have her. Grasping this pen and writing my hurt away. My hand can't move quickly enough. My fingers cramp up. My head is lowered in agony. My neck begs to be massaged. My back eagerly awaits for me to stand up and stretch. But this writing will continue until sweet slumber comes to me. I want her out of my head before I drift off into my R.E.M. She already consumes my conscious thoughts. I'll be damned if I give her my silent lucidity too. So, I write. Hand swift across this parchment. Ink staining the grain the same as her voice stained my ears. Her face stained my eyes. She made a stained mess of my heart and I can't find an eraser. I asked to have all of her. She said I can have half of her. Well, I want the half that her pain still grasps. The half that continues to punish me for what her exes still grasp. I want the half that fells and loves with reckless abandon. The half that gives and nurture, is faithful and true. The half that beats her heart and feeds her soul. I want that half of her that is reserved for special kisses and stolen glances, the half that ouches skin and whispers in ears. This half that she speaks of is her better half. Her loving half. Her living half. If I get that half then I'll surely give the same half and these two halves can be complete. It's been a ling time coming. I knew this pain was inevitable. Thought I was strong enough to withstand it. Turns out she made me weaker than I though I ever could be. She played me. She slayed me. These tears choke me. But water doesn't fall from these eyes. I hold it in. She won't see it happen. I cannot cry. I may be broken. But I've been here before and I have my own first aid whit which to mend myself. Music on. Lights down low. Drink in my left hand. Pen in my right hand. Clouds surrounding my head. I clear my head. Put pen to paper. Trying to forget her. Don't start my love if you can't handle my love. I don't give it away to just anyone. I'm choosy. I choose to be. To be me, loving you. I am your greatest loss. You gained nothing. I gained pain.

I chose you. I wanted you. I adored you. I admired you and cherished you. If I opened up why couldn't you have too? You weren't overwhelmed. Just under trusting. Unwilling to let go of the hurts from your past. So, now you punished me. You threw me away. Love wasted. Love deferred. Love unheard. So, with pen in my right hand, I etch out my sorrows swiftly with my write hand.

Her hues

She is a hand-painted ornament. Deep hues and ravishing lights, she is. Delicate. Crafted. Beauty in the flesh. Fragile, yet strong. She shines in the light. I proudly have her on display. Every day of the week. Every month of the year. I don't need a special occasion or a holiday to share her precious luster with the world. I make sure to shine her up every day. Making sure her etched beauty is shown in glorious display. I admire the highs and lows of her body. Taking in her curves. I see blues and reds. Warm greens and browns. When I wake up next to her, I see her sparkle in the sunlight. And at night, her nakedness twinkles in the moonlight leaving me breathless. She is my hand-painted ornament. Deep hues. Ravishing lights, she is. Delicate. Crafted. Beautiful flesh. I am honored that she shares her precious luster in my world.

Dandylion

I wanted to write her a sweet poem to express
how much she means to me. About how, at this
time in my life, her presence has made me smile
ear to ear. About how her touch and her kiss
sends chills all over my body; at this time in my
life. About how day after day I sit and wait and
count the days until we see each other again.
About how her face lights up the darkest areas of
my heart. About how I love to run my fingers
through her big, lion's mane of hair. About how
she is quite possibly the best thing since Tracy
and Fast Car. About how I imagine and
reimagine our brief rendezvous spent together.
About how I can't seem to focus on anyone else
but her. About how much I wish our
circumstances were different, About how I wish
I was her alpha. Not her once-in-a-while, catch a
flight, meet me in a random city, weekend beta.
But, I can't write that poem because she chose to
marry someone else and I have been reduced to
omega and she will never know my heartbreak,
at this time.

Ominous

Tired. More than sleepy. Quiet slumber. Exhausted and spent. I zone out. TV on in the back, but I don't hear it. Good night, my dearest. There are words stuck in my throat. I've been venting. NO escape from my conviction. I've got an ominous feeling. Something unpleasant is going to happen. Threatening. Inauspicious. But, I let my words speak. Speak of freedom. Oh, sweet glory and transformation. No more of love's oppression. I can guarantee.

Between

I am in between spaces. Just gliding. Fortunate for light travel. I can move through these stars. Brilliant. Light bending. Moonlight. Clusters of meaning. Absorbing shine.

I blew an amp

I choke every day from the words stuck in my throat. I can't ever scream loud enough. Not a soul hears me. I am nothing. Muted. Millions of words a day never pass through these lips. They stay sheltered by tongue. Idle. I can never speak if such things. NO sweet reward of linguistic artistry. So, I swallow them back down. Spiraling. Down. Gone. Stifled. Until...I blew an amp. I sang too bright. My voice could not be contained. Speakers now can't hold my words.

Far beyond

Evolve. Elevate. We're on this higher echelon.
Meet me in the galaxies. Far beyond
comprehension.

Moon don't shine

Moon, don't shine for me. I won't appreciate your sparkle. You see, my woman, she left me. She said I was overwhelming and too difficult. But she was unvaried and dull. She kissed me one last time under your midnight gaze. I don't know how to bask in your glow now. All I feel when I see you is pain, regret, and hurt. I am angry at you , Moon. You led her a path away from me with your radiance that night.

She is

So, she becomes my home. She is the place where earth and water meet. She is where trees sway and wind leaves me breathless. Shaky ground no more. She is but a foundation of hope and courage. She is the moonlit corners of my dark heart's rooms. She wakes me up for twilight lovemaking. She is glistening shadows from the sun's morning stretch and dance. She is my place of joy. She is my final nesting place.

I just am

In a life before, I was a beatnik. Maybe a revolutionary. I am a city girl with a southern soul. I walk around barefoot and love my high heels. I believe in philanthropy and entrepreneurship. June Cleaver and Tupperware with some Stonewall and Paris is Burning. I want to sit on my wrap around porch and sip sweet tea, with bourbon, and mint juleps. But I am akin to late night dance clubbin' and finger snappin' spoken word nights. I am bacon and butter and sushi and quinoa. I am an aggressive femme, high tops and basketball shorts, combat boots and a black beret with an evening gown and diamonds, some bamboo earrings (at least two pair), tattoos and white gloves, Mary Jane and Newport menthols with namaste and Nam Myoho Renge Kyo. I just am.

Unwelcome

I am not here for your pleasure. I am here for mine. Love, you are unwelcomed. Unwanted. Unappreciated.

Farewell

Goodbye. I had hoped you would stay longer.
But, I understand. You do this to me every time.
Farwell, Love. You won't be missed. You never
are.

Signed, Love

Dear reader, I have no potential. I am lazy. Unmoved. Unimpressed. Selfish. Speak my name, but I will never be yours. Signed, Love.

Peace

I don't love in black & white. I love in color. With shapes and puzzles. Pick me up. Figure me out. Try and put me back together. Match those jagged edges. Make sure those pieces fit. Is the full picture clear yet? My heart peace is missing and can never be found. But, still, put me back together with what peace I have left.

Signed, Me

Dear Love, I didn't want you to begin with. But, you pushed your way in. Now, you've left abruptly. So, you can stay away. I didn't want you anyway. Signed, Me

Shallow

Stop deep diving. I am all surface. Superficial.
Vain. No conscious. I will ruin you. My name is
Love.

This moment

Tonight I am not giving in to my normal crying, heartache ritual. The next eight hours will be vested to sweet slumber. I am not in chaos at the moment.

Sucka free

I remain free. No shackles of love here. I broke those confines years ago.

Be kept

Am I not deserving? Have I not earned every little bit? Where's my adoration? My adulation? My consummation? I pursued. I wooed. I spent precious energy. I gave my time. I gave my body. I gave my soul. You, again, are fleeing, saying you can't be kept. Who needs love anyway?

To Love

Shackle my heart if you must. As long as my
mind is free. You can never have me

Mecca

You will rise while nighttime stars still shine. I am at ease. My whispers are slow. Your breath is hot. Life and love are elevated. We rise. We soar. We float together into this infinite space. At our mutual apex, our azure light cannot escape. Deep hues and ravishing lights you are. Your flesh on my flesh, as we culminate in this ecstasy and glory. We weep in the midst of our rhapsody in Shangri-La. Our summits enrapture us in a stratosphere to an unknown zenith. My ether. My everlasting. My Mecca.